AF362065

Join my newsletter and get
my ebook library for FREE!

INGO BLUM

Where Is My Little Elephant?

Wo ist mein kleiner Elefant?

ENGLISH/GERMAN

Where is Daisy, my little elephant?

Wo ist Daisy, mein kleiner Elefant?

She is not in the china shop.

Sie ist nicht im Porzellanladen.

She is not in the circus.

Sie ist nicht im Zirkus.

There are many animals there.
But no elephant!

Dort sind viele Tiere.

Aber kein Elefant!

Isn't today her birthday?

Ist heute nicht ihr Geburtstag?

Perhaps she is with
her friends!

Vielleicht ist sie mit

ihren Freunden

zusammen!

10

Is she at the ice rink?

Ist sie auf der Eislaufbahn?

No, there is no
elephant on that ice.

Nein, da ist kein

Elefant auf dem Eis.

12
MoNKeY

She is not at the zoo.

Sie ist nicht im Zoo.

The animals miss her.

Die Tiere

vermissen sie.

14

She is not standing
under the tree.

Sie steht nicht unter dem Baum.

Is she hiding?

Versteckt sie sich?

16

Is she making music?
Macht sie Musik?

No. Elephants cannot play
a musical instrument.
Nein. Elefanten können
kein Musikinstrument
spielen.

She is not at school.

Sie ist nicht in der Schule.

Is Daisy lazy?

Ist Daisy faul?

20

Look, there she is!

Schau, dort ist sie!

Daisy is on a ship with her friends, a lion and a rhino.

Daisy ist auf einem Schiff mit ihren Freunden, einem Löwen und einem Nashorn.

Color the elephant.

Mal den Elefanten aus.

More Reading and Coloring Fun

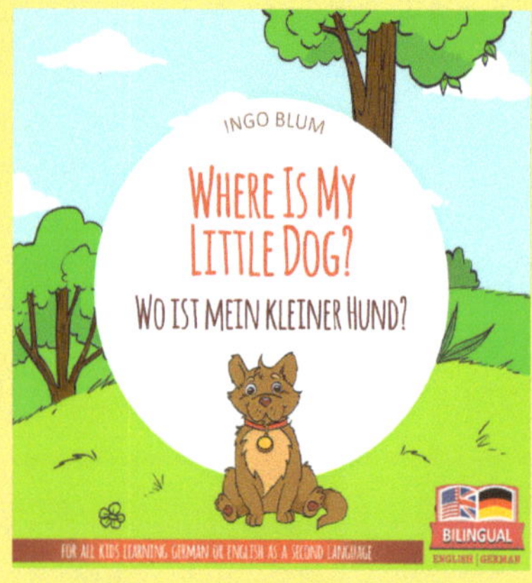

ISBN 978-1-982925-46-8

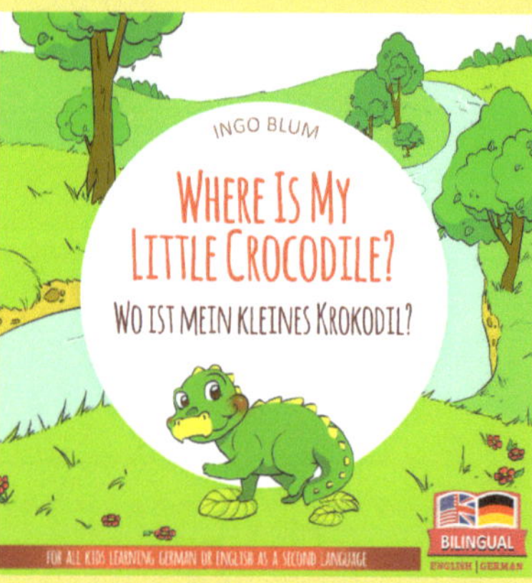

ISBN 978-1-982922-57-3

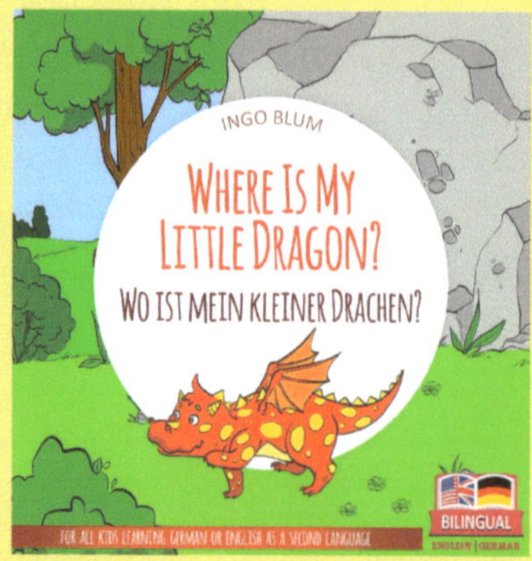

ISBN 978-1-982924-05-8

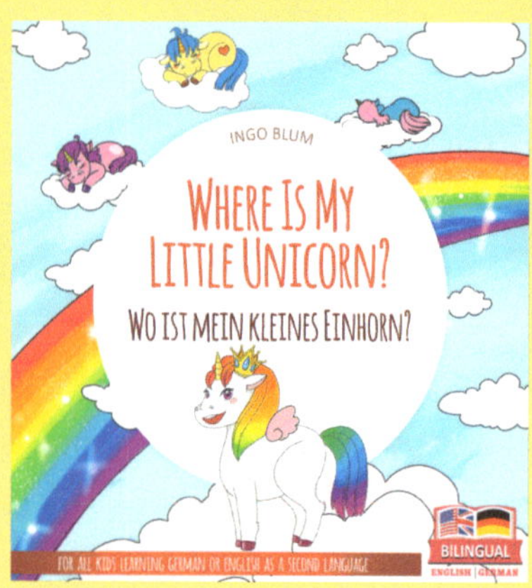

ISBN 979-8-460931-34-7

ISBN 978-1-983093-97-5

ISBN 979-8-682547-90-6

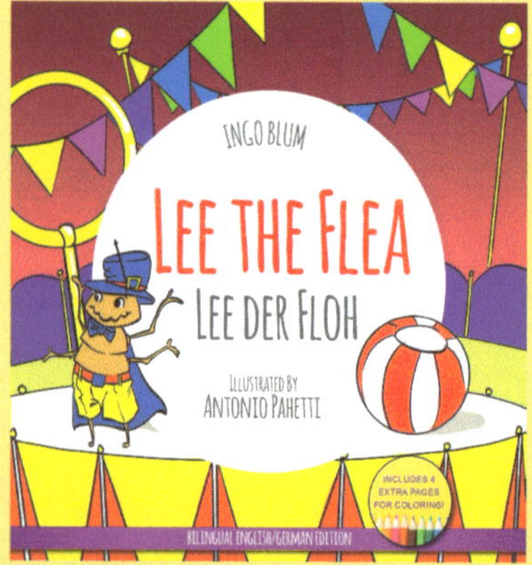

ISBN 978-1-790104-73-4

ISBN 979-8-672025-68-1

ISBN 978-1-982925-84-0